ENGLISH

TEN STE
to improve you

WRITING
for ages 8-9

Let's learn at home

AUTHOR Sue Palmer

ILLUSTRATOR Phil Dobson

Improve your presentation

Presentation is all about how good your work looks – for instance, how it's set out on the page, how it's illustrated and how neat it is.

The most important part of presentation is handwriting. It should be neat and easy to read.

It should be easy to write as well!

Go over these handwriting patterns with coloured pens or pencils, and finish each line.
Do the outer patterns first, turning the page round as you go, so you're always writing from left to right. Then do the inner patterns the same way.

▼

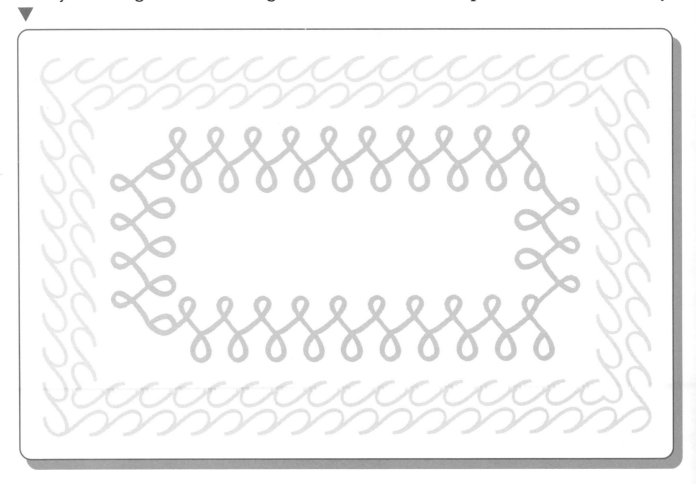

Copy these rhymes in your best joined handwriting.

▼

I wish I were a little bug

_____

With whiskers on my tummy.

_____

I'd climb into the honey pot

_____

And make my tummy gummy.

_____

A canner exceedingly canny

_____

One morning remarked to his granny,

_____

'A canner can can

_____

Anything that he can,

_____

But a canner can't can a can can he?'

_____

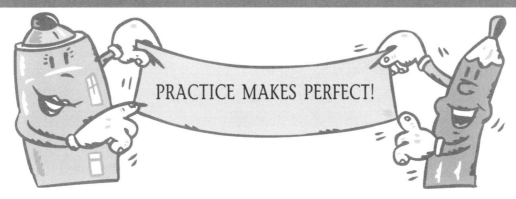

PRACTICE MAKES PERFECT!

Now turn over

HEADINGS LOOK GOOD IN CAPITAL LETTERS

Plan the layout of your work in advance, particularly for factual writing.

You can rub guidelines out later, if you want.

If the paper isn't lined, make your own pencil lines for headings. Always use a ruler!

Go over the capital letters with coloured pens or pencils.
Then copy them neatly (in another colour) in the box below.
▼

A B C D E F G H I J K L M N O P Q R S T U V W X Y Z

The heading for this writing should be 'How to set out information text'. Write it in.

In information text, use different sorts of writing style for different purposes, for example:

HEADINGS   Capital letters, colour or underlining help make headings stand out. They draw your reader's attention to what the page is about.

<u>**subheadings**</u>   Smaller capitals or underlining show that subheadings are important, but not as important as the main heading.

captions and labels   Print script makes these quick and easy to read, and shows that they are separate from the rest of your writing.

Copy these sentences to practise different sorts of writing.

▼

THESE ARE LARGE CAPITALS FOR IMPORTANT HEADINGS

_____

_____

SMALL CAPITALS ARE GOOD FOR SUBHEADINGS KEEP THEM ALL THE SAME HEIGHT

_____

_____

Print script is suitable for captions and labels because it is clear and easy to read.

_____

_____

_____

_____

_____

_____

Don't use print script for all your writing because it takes much longer than joined writing.

When you finish this step put a sticker here!

Dear Parent or Carer

All written work is easier for children if their handwriting is neat and fluent. Neat work is also easier for teachers and examiners to read, which can make a difference to the way work is marked! Encourage your child to practise handwriting and artwork which develops hand control. Good clear layout makes a great difference to work – encourage your child's attention to detail in his or her work. Answers on page 30.

Guide readers with punctuation

Punctuation marks show where the reader should pause to break the text into meaningful chunks, and they can also show different sorts of sentences and the tone of voice required.

WELCOME TO PUNCTUATION STREET
Practise the first verse of
The Punctuation Street rap!

I'm at the end of **exclamations** – sentences that want to be noticed! Exclamations are cool!

If I'm at the end of a sentence, it's called a **statement**. (Policemen are always taking statements.)

STATEMENT

Can you recognise a **question**? And do you know what I'm called?

I'm sometimes at the end of a sentence, but I don't finish it off – I just ...

There are three punctuation marks that can finish a sentence (and one that can show a sentence is unfinished).

WHEN A SENTENCE IS UNFINISHED ...

Put **.** **?** **!** or **...** at the end of these speeches.

▼

The treasure is in the

Oh no – now we'll never know

What's going on

Long John's parrot has just died

Opposite is the last entry in ▶
the cabin boy's diary.
Use **.** **?** **!** or **...** to split this text
into sentences. Remember to
start each new sentence with
a capital letter.

Now read the diary entry
aloud, following your
punctuation.
Does it guide you in:
• breaking the text into
meaningful chunks?
• adjusting your tone of
voice?

Long John Brasso's favourite parrot died today when Long John passed away last month, who would have guessed the parrot would follow him so soon the poor bird never got over the death of its master
Everyone thinks Long John's secret died with the bird but they're wrong Long John told one other person where the treasure was buried he told me would anyone believe a young ship's cabin boy could have such a secret
Yes I know where to find the treasure it is buried in the

1ST SPEAKER:	Inkypinky wobble-bobble-flop?
2ND SPEAKER:	Wobble-wobble-wobble.
1ST SPEAKER:	Ooby-jooby!
2ND SPEAKER:	Wobble-bobble-flop inky-pink?
1ST SPEAKER:	Bobbly-floppity-floo...
2ND SPEAKER:	Gook! Gook!
1ST SPEAKER:	Inkypinky twiddle-flob. Floppit.

▲

This conversation makes no sense, but you can
work out how it should sound just from the
punctuation. Read it aloud with a friend.

All the punctuation marks
Are writers' little friends,
But only we, the important three,
Can show where a sentence ends!

Now turn over

We guide readers round a sentence, showing where to breathe.

Commas are small, not very strong, but extremely helpful.

But they're not strong enough to finish a sentence.

Once upon a time there was a little wasp called Buzz ◯ he lived in a nest at the bottom of a garden with his brothers ◯ who were called Fuzz ◯ Wuzz and Muzz ◯ one summer's day ◯ they decided to go on a picnic ◯ Fuzz ◯ Wuzz and Muzz wanted to go to the seaside ◯ so they packed their buckets ◯ spades and picnic basket and set off ◯ at last they arrived at the sea ◯ only to discover that the beach was packed with people ◯ there was no room for even the teeniest little wasp to squash in ◯ sadly ◯ Buzz ◯ Fuzz ◯ Wuzz and Muzz set off back home ◯ muttering that people always turn up and spoil your picnics ◯

▲

In this text, boxes show missing punctuation marks. Choose a comma or a full stop each time. If you choose a full stop, give the next word a capital letter.

Practise the second verse of
The Punctuation Street rap!

I'm a **hyphen**. I stick words together with my cut-and-stick outfit.

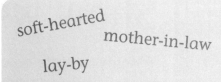

soft-hearted
mother-in-law
lay-by

Dashes keep words apart, but hyphens stick them together!

We separate words off from the rest of the sentence with our crooks (also known as **brackets**).

We can keep the words apart – no trouble! A full stop's too final but a comma's not enough? Try a **dash**.

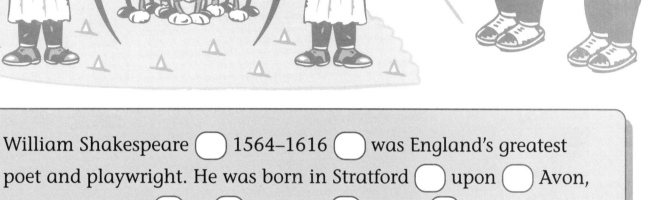

William Shakespeare ◯ 1564–1616 ◯ was England's greatest poet and playwright. He was born in Stratford ◯ upon ◯ Avon, the son of a well ◯ to ◯ do glove ◯ maker ◯ an important man in the town. At 18, William married a local girl ◯ Ann Hathaway ◯ but soon left Stratford to seek his fortune in London ◯ England's capital city.

▲ Boxes show missing punctuation marks. Choose a dash, hyphen or bracket each time.

When you finish this step put a sticker here!

Dear Parent or Carer

Punctuation marks are a poor substitute for the tones and rhythms of the human voice, but they are all the writer has. Help your child respond to them when reading – this is the best way to learn their use. Answers on pages 30 and 31.

Show who's talking

When you write down the exact words someone says, it's called **direct speech**.

Practise the third verse of **The Punctuation Street rap**!

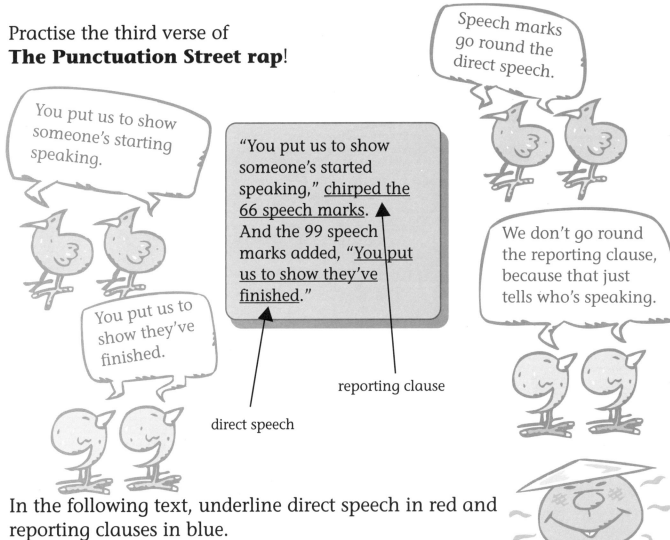

Speech marks go round the direct speech.

You put us to show someone's starting speaking.

"You put us to show someone's started speaking," chirped the 66 speech marks. And the 99 speech marks added, "You put us to show they've finished."

We don't go round the reporting clause, because that just tells who's speaking.

You put us to show they've finished.

reporting clause

direct speech

In the following text, underline direct speech in red and reporting clauses in blue.

▼

The teacher asked, "Which is the farthest away – China or the sun?"

"China," answered Milly.

"Why do you think that?" asked the teacher in surprise.

"Well, you can see the sun, but you can't see China," Milly replied.

Go over the speech marks and all capital letters and punctuation marks inside the speech marks in red.
Go over any punctuation marks and capital letters outside the speech marks in blue.

How's my singing coming on, Miss Jones?

I think you should be on TV, Sam.

Really? You mean I'm good enough for that?

No, but if you were on TV I could switch you off.

Write the conversation from the cartoon strip as direct speech. You will have to add in direct speech punctuation and reporting clauses.

▼

_____

_____

_____

_____

_____

_____

_____

_____

_____

_____

_____

_____

_____

_____

_____

_____

RULES FOR DIRECT SPEECH

- Start each new speaker on a new line.
- Put speech marks round the words actually spoken.
- Place punctuation connected with the direct speech **inside** the speech marks.
- Separate direct speech from reporting clauses with a comma (or **?** or **!** if direct speech is a question or exclamation).

When you finish this step put a sticker here!

Dear Parent or Carer

It can take a long time to learn all the rules for direct speech. The rules above are given in order of importance. If your child finds it difficult, take the rules one at a time. Give plenty of practice until he or she feels confident of one rule, then introduce the next. Answers on page 31.

Use adjectives and adverbs

Detail and description make writing come alive. You need **describing words** to help your reader imagine exactly what you mean.

The little black and white dog was growling playfully.

The enormous guard dog was growling fiercely.

▲

Underline the extra words that have been used in each sentence.

_____   _____

_____   _____

▲

Add the same number of extra words to the sentences above.
Choose words which fill in the detail each time.

Draw pictures of two very different monsters to illustrate this sentence. Make them roar in very different ways!

Write two sentences based on **The monster roared** to describe your two pictures.

The monster roared.

If you're looking for good describing words, find a thesaurus.

THESAURUS

In the sentences you wrote on pages 12 and 13, you used two kinds of describing words – adjectives and adverbs.

Adjectives are describing words. They tell you what someone or something is like.

Write good **adjectives** to complete these sentences.

▼

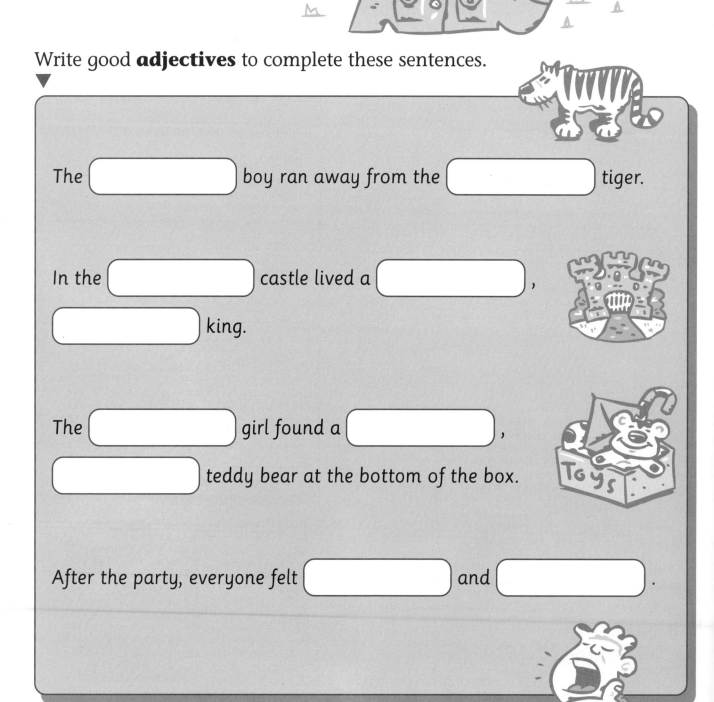

The [   ] boy ran away from the [   ] tiger.

In the [   ] castle lived a [   ],

[   ] king.

The [   ] girl found a [   ],

[   ] teddy bear at the bottom of the box.

After the party, everyone felt [   ] and [   ].

14

Adverbs can tell you **how** something happens.

THE ADVERB GAME

You need at least two players. One player is IT and leaves the room. The rest decide on an adverb of manner (for instance, **noisily**). IT comes in and gives tasks to the others, such as:
sing a song
brush your teeth
eat something
open the door.
They must do the tasks **in the manner of the adverb**. IT has to guess the adverb.

The cat walked [   ] across the steep roof.

People talk [   ] in a library.

SSHH

Matthew stroked his pet rabbit [   ].

The cars raced [   ] round the track.

The old man spoke [   ] to the dog who had

just trampled on his flowers.

When you finish this step put a sticker here!

▲
Write good **adverbs** to finish these sentences.

Dear Parent or Carer

Help your child notice adjectives and adverbs when you read together, and discuss how they improve the writing. Encourage your child to add descriptive words to bring his or her own writing to life. Answers on page 31.

Improve your vocabulary

We need words to express what we mean. The more words you know, the better and clearer your writing will be.

How good is your vocabulary? Here's your chance to find out.

For each of these words, three possible meanings have been given. One is correct, the others are wrong. Tick the one you think is right each time.

various (adjective)
- [ ] wonderful
- [ ] different
- [ ] old and tired

distort (verb)
- [ ] twist out of shape
- [ ] chew up
- [ ] take to school

crisis (noun)
- [ ] the shape of a cross
- [ ] a very difficult time
- [ ] a loud noise

optimist (noun)
- [ ] someone with a sore leg
- [ ] an eye-doctor
- [ ] someone who expects good things to happen

chronic (adjective)
- [ ] going on for a long time
- [ ] very bad
- [ ] tired and weak

competent (adjective)
- [ ] good-looking
- [ ] angry
- [ ] good at what you are doing

deceive (verb)
- [ ] collect
- [ ] write a letter
- [ ] cheat, lie to someone

pessimist (noun)
- [ ] large furry animal
- [ ] someone who expects bad things to happen
- [ ] someone who tries hard

Use a dictionary to check whether you are right.

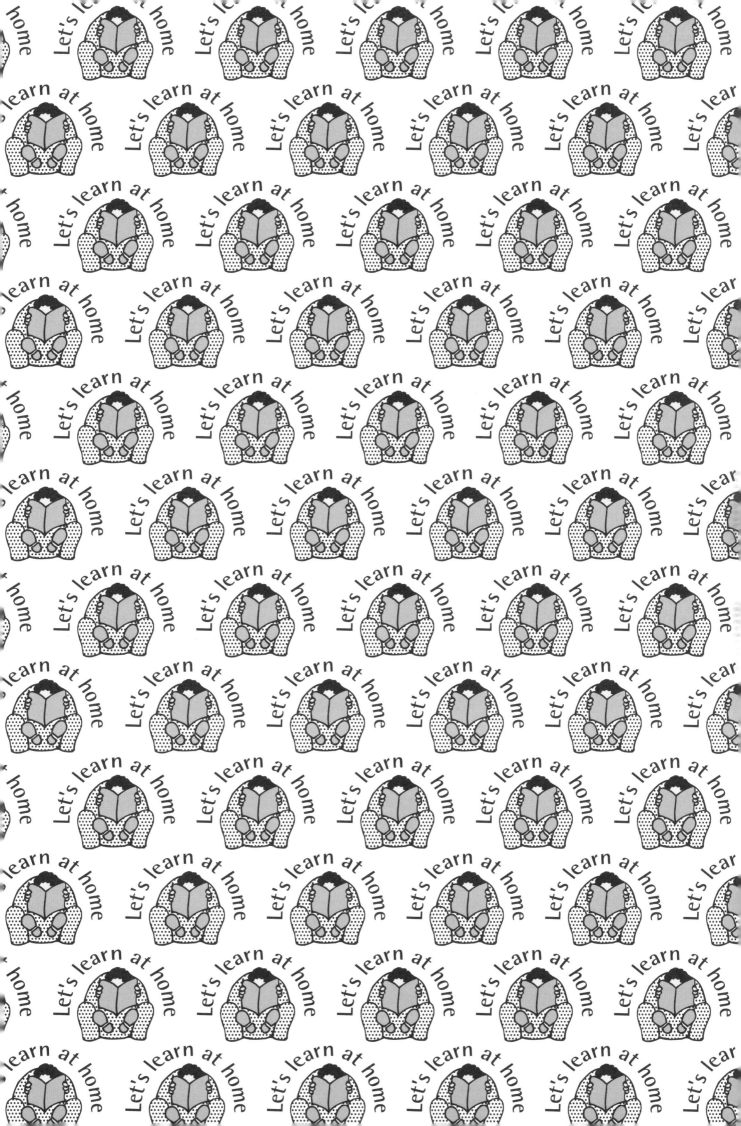

The Punctuation Street rap

You gotta punk and chunk to make that text make sense –
You gotta put a full stop after every sentence.
An exclamation mark for exclamation!!
A curly question mark for interrogation.
Three dots show that it's incomplete...
That's how to chunk text on Punctuation Street.

You gotta punk and chunk to make those sentences clear –
Commas show the way around your ideas,
You want to hold words apart – a dash can hack it –
(To cordon them off, you need brackets.)

You gotta punk and chunk those spoken words
With the speech marks showing what is overheard.
Help your readers know which are the spoken lines
With those sixty-sixes and ninety-nines.
Commas hold back reporting clauses, nice and neat,
To chunk direct speech on Punctuation Street.

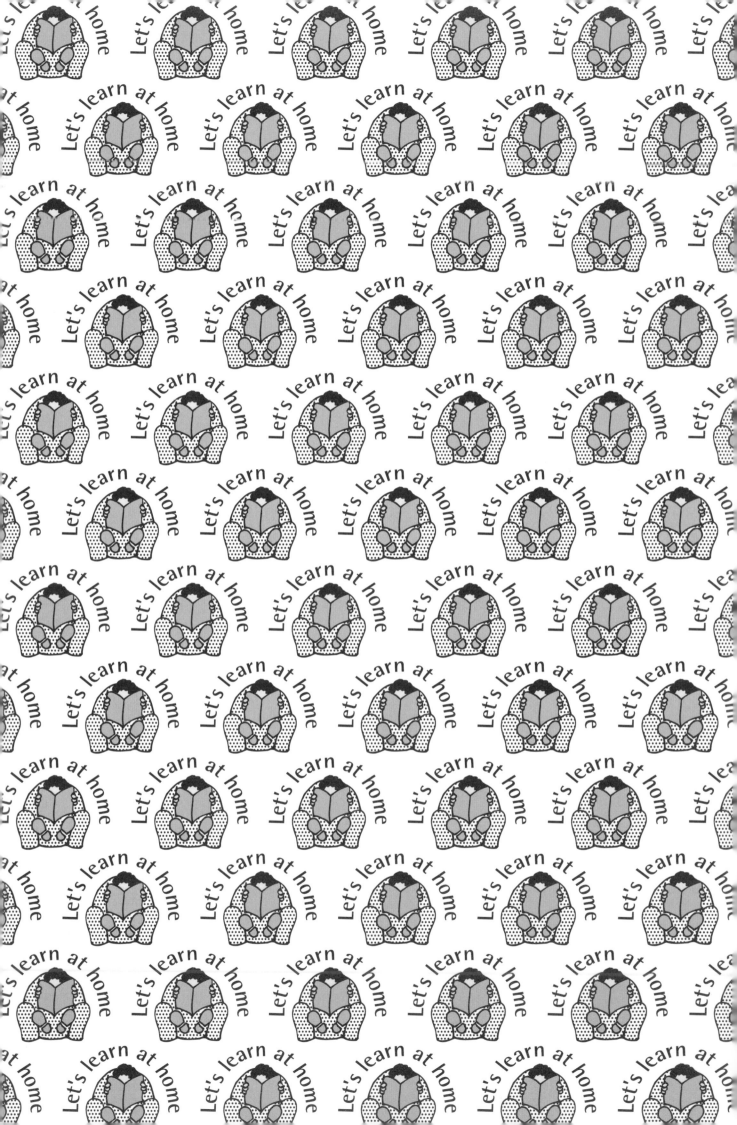

WORD OF THE DAY

Try to learn one new word every day.

- Find a new word each day in the dictionary.
- Make sure you know what it means and how to spell it.
- Use it in a sentence.
- Try to use the word in two ways during the day:
    – when you are talking;
    – in your writing (if it will fit!).

Make sure you know the meaning of the words on page 16.
Choose the best one to finish each sentence.

▼

The man suffered for years with a

[   ] illness.

Bad weather can sometimes

[   ] the picture on the TV

screen.

The wolf tried to [   ] Little

Red Riding Hood, but she saw through

his plan.

'Twixt optimist and pessimist

The difference is droll:

The [   ] sees the doughnut,

The [   ] sees the hole!

When you finish this step put a sticker here!

Dear Parent or Carer

The wider a child's vocabulary, the better his or her writing. Help your child to use a children's dictionary to look up the meanings of words. Another good way to improve your child's vocabulary is to read to him or her. Choose books which are a bit too hard for your child to read alone. Answers on page 31.

Take care with apostrophes

Apostrophes are punctuation marks **inside** words and they are used in two important ways: either to show that letters have been missed out, or that someone owns something.

man

woman

stall

It's the **owner** who gets the apostrophe.

tail

Complete the following.

The hat belonging to the man = the man's hat.

The [   ] belonging to the [   ] = the man's stall.

The bag belonging to the [   ] = [   ].

The [   ] belonging to the dog = [   ].

Write an **apostrophe phrase** for these.

The pet belonging to Mark = _____

The wing belonging to the bird = _____

The idea belonging to Rachel = _____

18

Some people stick apostrophes all over the place. You often see them on market stalls.

TOMATO'S
BANANA'S
CABBAGE'S

In each of these sentences, one apostrophe is correct and one is wrong. Give the correct apostrophe a tick, and put a cross after the wrong one.

Don't forget the apostrophe can also show that letters have been missed out.

Complete this chart.

▼

Short form	Long form	Letters missed out
haven't		
	does not	
couldn't		
would've		
	did not	
	might have	
	I have	
we'll		
you're		
	it is	

▶

The queen's ◯ cat's ◯ were yowling in the yard.

We had burger's ◯ and chips at Ian's ◯ party.

The farmer's ◯ potatoes were stored in sack's ◯.

Hundred's ◯ of people were at the ship's ◯ launch.

If the owner already ends in **s** (because it's plural), you just put the apostrophe on the end.

the dog's bone   the dogs' bone

▲

Can you spot the difference?

When you finish this step put a sticker here!

Dear Parent or Carer

The apostrophe is the most misused punctuation mark. Make sure your child understands the rules in this step. If you spot any wrongly used apostrophes when you're out and about, point them out to your child – other people's mistakes can be a powerful aid to learning! Answers on page 31.

Get your facts in order

When you're writing, work out what you want to say first to make sure you get things in the right order. This is especially important when you're writing non-fiction.

Instructions are a sort of non-fiction writing. Instructions have to be very clear indeed, so the reader knows exactly what they mean.

If you make a rough plan before you write, it helps you get the order really clear.

Plan

1 _____

2 _____

3 _____

◀ You are going to write instructions for making a cup of tea. Talk about how it's done with an adult, and jot down notes in the planning frame (left). Add as many extra stages as you need.

As you plan, you may have to change things, or add things in.

Don't worry if it gets messy – they're only rough notes.

When you know exactly what you want to say:
- read the box below
- write your instructions. ▶

Good linking words
Start each new point with a good linking word (or group of words).
These words act like signposts. They tell the reader that you have finished one point and are going on to the next.

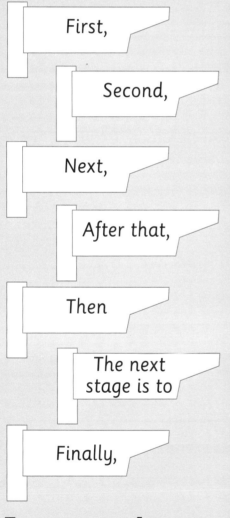

First,

Second,

Next,

After that,

Then

The next stage is to

Finally,

Try not to use **then** too often. Use other linking words instead. Try never to use **and then** – it doesn't sound good!

HOW TO MAKE A CUP OF TEA

When you finish this step put a sticker here!

Dear Parent or Carer

Ordering one's thoughts doesn't come naturally, but it helps to think things through before writing. Talking something through is a good preparation – encourage your child to tell you what he or she is going to write before writing it. Rough notes also help, and they provide a framework for writing. Answers on page 32.

Keep to the standard

At home or with their friends, people often speak non-standard English, but you should always write in **standard English**.

In each sentence, a word or phrase is non-standard. Rewrite each sentence in standard English, using the words from the box.

very fashionable	disappointed
ill enormous	very pleased

Jake was gutted when his team lost the game.

_____

I'm well chuffed about my exam result.

_____

Emma looks fab in her new clothes.

_____

There was a ginormous parcel in the hall.

_____

Will went home because he felt conkered.

_____

Adverbs of manner tell you **how** something happens.
Anna writes very **slowly**. ✓

In non-standard English, people often use adjectives instead of adverbs.
Anna writes very **slow**. ✗

Rewrite each sentence in standard English.
▼

The group played brilliant.

_____

Why do you always shout real loud?

_____

Everyone should sit quiet and wait.

_____

Get ready quick or you'll be late.

_____

When you're talking about yourself and other people, it's polite to put them first.

Me and Alex played football. ✗
Alex and I played football. ✓

Rewrite each sentence in standard English.
▼

Me and my dad go out every Saturday.

_____

Me and you should see the team.

_____

_____

When you finish this step put a sticker here!

Dear Parent or Carer

The most common differences between standard and non-standard English are small points of grammar, and occasionally vocabulary. Accent doesn't matter – you can speak English with any accent, as long as the grammar is standard. Answers on page 32.

Choose the right style

There are lots of different styles of writing. For instance, your writing style can be **formal** or **informal**, depending on why you're writing and who is going to read it.

When I am writing a letter to someone I don't know very well, I use a formal style.

But when I'm writing to my friend, I'm much more informal.

Read these two letters, then answer the quiz on page 25.

25 November 1998

Formality House
Style Road
WRITTENHAND
KS2 3RS

Dear Sir
   I'm afraid I have a complaint to make about one of your products. Along with this letter I am enclosing the remains of a bar of 'Krunchykrisp' which I bought this weekend at a garage in the village of Barley in Wiltshire.
   According to your advertisements, 'Krunchykrisp' is 'crunchy, munchy and punchy' but, as I am sure you will agree, the bar I bought does not live up to this description. In fact, it is soft and rather disgusting.
   I am returning the bar, as I'm sure your company would not wish customers to be supplied with faulty products. I hope you will be prepared to refund my postage and the cost of the bar.

Yours faithfully

Ivor Complaint

Ivor Complaint

25/11/98

Dear Josh,
   Just a note to say how fed up I was to miss you on Saturday! Sorry we were late – the car broke down. We were stuck for ages while Dad tried to get it fixed. The only food the garage sold was Krunchykrisp bars, and the one I bought was all gooey and yucky! It wasn't a good day at all!
   Still, Ravi says you'll be back next month. Let's hope we meet up then.
Looking forward to seeing you,
Love,
Ivor

FORMAL LETTER STYLE

INFORMAL LETTER STYLE

FORMAL V INFORMAL QUIZ

Write these descriptions in the correct box – **formal letter style** or **informal letter style**:

- full address in top left-hand corner

- shortened address

- full date

- short form of date

- Start: Dear Sir/Madam/Mr.../Mrs.../Ms...

- Start: Dear... and the person's first name

- Sign off: Yours sincerely/Yours faithfully

- Sign off: Best wishes/Love/Cheers – or whatever you like!

FORMAL LANGUAGE

INFORMAL LANGUAGE

It's not just the way you set out a letter that makes it formal or informal, it's the words you choose and the way you put them together.

If you know the person's name you can write **Dear Mr...** or **Dear Mrs/Ms...** and you should sign off **Yours sincerely.** If you don't know their name you should write **Dear Sir...** or **Dear Madam...** and sign off **Yours faithfully**.

Read the letters on page 24 again and do the **Formal v informal quiz (Part 2)** below. Write your answers in the boxes.

FORMAL V INFORMAL QUIZ (PART 2)

Write these descriptions in the correct box – **formal language** or **informal language**.

- lots of long words
- mostly shorter words
- words written out in full
- shortened forms like **I'm**, **wasn't** and so on
- long sentences
- short, snappy sentences
- sounds like everyday speech
- sounds less chatty than everyday speech
- main punctuation – full stops and commas
- more use of dashes and exclamation marks.

_____

_____

_____

_____

_____

_____

_____

_____

_____

_____

_____

_____

_____

_____

_____

_____

_____

_____

When you finish this step put a sticker here!

▲

Write either a **formal** letter (a complaint to your headteacher about something that you don't like about school) or an **informal** letter (to someone you know well, telling them what you've been doing recently).

Dear Parent or Carer

Letters are a good way of demonstrating degrees of formality and informality in writing. Help your child recognise that we use different layouts and formats, and choose different words and expressions, depending on why we're writing and who we expect to read our work. Help your child notice this in everyday reading and writing. Discuss the letters your child has written – do they follow the rules? Answers on page 32.

Proofread your work

Whenever you have finished writing anything, **always** read it to check for mistakes, then correct it.

There's so much to think about when you're writing – spelling, handwriting, punctuation… if you're not careful, you can forget what you have to say!

GET IDEAS DOWN FIRST, THEN CHECK YOUR WORK.

The first thing to check is that your work makes sense.
• Read it **aloud** to yourself to see where it needs breaking up, and add any missing punctuation.
• You may also wish to add in extra information to improve the writing.

The second thing to check is the spelling.
Check for spelling mistakes at the end of every piece of writing.

How to proofread for spelling
• As you read through, underline the words you think are wrong.
• Check these words. Try them on a piece of scrap paper.
• If you think you're right, cross out the mistake and write the correct spelling neatly above it.
• If you're not sure, check in a dictionary or spellchecker, or ask an adult.

Or you can check it whenever you need a little breather from thinking what to write!

This newspaper report needs proofreading! Check it and underline all the mistakes. Write the corrections above them.

▼

CAKE CRISIS – SHOCK HORROR!

All readers will know Mr jones newtowns popular baker. Mr Jones has a problem he hasent got enyone to mind his shop when he gose on holiday nexed week. if he doesent find someone there will be no bred or cakes on sale all week if you wood like to take over mr jones's shop plees right to him at 11 High street, newtown.

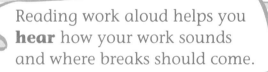

Reading work aloud helps you **hear** how your work sounds and where breaks should come.

It can also help to swap work with a friend. It's easier to spot mistakes in someone else's work!

When you finish this step put a sticker here!

Dear Parent or Carer

Encourage your child to get his or her thoughts on paper in clear, interesting ways. Then tell your child to check it through – suggest he or she reads it aloud to you, and help to find and correct the errors. Answers on page 32.

Parents' pages

Speaking and writing

Speaking comes naturally to human beings; writing doesn't. In order to write their ideas down, children must learn many skills. Some of these – like handwriting – are obvious, some less so. The ten steps in this book tackle skills which are particularly important at this stage in children's writing development.

Organising their thoughts

We don't need to think (much!) before we speak, because we don't need to speak in perfect sentences, and we can adjust and add to our meaning as we go along. But to make sense to a reader, writing has to be:
- in complete sentences;
- planned and organised;
- set out according to accepted rules.

Children must learn to *think* about how they are using language (see Steps 7 and 9).

Following the rules

Writing involves learning many rules of handwriting, punctuation, standard English and various conventions of layout. Children also have to learn important rules and patterns of spelling – these are covered in the *Ten Steps to Improve your Child's Spelling* series.

Once children are aware of the rules, they need plenty of practice until they come automatically (see Steps 1, 2, 3, 6, 8 and 10).

Choosing their words

The point of writing is to get your message across to the reader as clearly as possible. This means:
- choosing words carefully;
- putting in enough description to help your readers 'see' what you mean;
- providing 'signposts' to your readers to demarcate different pieces of information.

For this, children need a wide vocabulary. One of the most important things you can do to help your child with writing is to help him or her learn more and more words (see Steps 4 and 5). Dictionaries and thesauruses help, but the two best ways for children to enlarge their vocabulary are talking with adults and reading good books.

Reading and writing

The more a child reads, the better he or she will write. Reading good books:
- increases children's vocabulary;
- teaches standard English grammar;

- gives them examples of different styles and effective descriptions;
- makes children familiar with the rhythms of language that underlie punctuation.

There are suggestions for improving your child's reading skills in the *Ten Steps to Improve your Child's Reading* series.

Different types of writing

Children tend to think of writing as being about 'stories', either fictional stories or true ones about their own experience. In fact, there are many other types of writing which are just as important in their own way, for example shopping lists, letters and notes, instructions and other sorts of factual information.

Try to give your child experience of reading and writing many different types of written material. Opportunities crop up all the time, in the reading and writing we have to do for everyday life. Involving children in real-life reading and writing also helps them see the point of learning all the skills involved.

 Step 1 Improve your presentation

Pages 2–3: Children trace over handwriting patterns that require the page to be turned and practise their handwriting by copying rhymes.

Pages 4–5: Children practise writing different types of writing styles.

 Step 2 Guide readers with punctuation

Pages 6–7: The treasure is in the...
Oh no – now we'll never know!
What's going on?
Long John's parrot has just died.

> Long John Brasso's favourite parrot died today. When Long John passed away last month, who would have guessed the parrot would follow him so soon? The poor bird never got over the death of its master.
> Everyone thinks Long John's secret died with the bird but they're wrong. Long John told one other person where the treasure was buried. He told me! Would anyone believe a young ship's cabin boy could have such a secret?
> Yes! I know where to find the treasure. It is buried in the...

Pages 8–9: Once upon a time there was a little wasp called Buzz. He lived in a nest at the bottom of a garden with his brothers, who were called Fuzz, Wuzz and Muzz. One summer's day, they decided to go on a picnic. Fuzz, Wuzz and Muzz wanted to go to the seaside, so they packed their buckets, spades and picnic basket and set off. At last they arrived at the sea, only to discover that the beach was packed with people. There was no room for even the teeniest little wasp to squash in. Sadly, Buzz, Fuzz, Wuzz and Muzz set off back home, muttering that people always turn up and spoil your picnic.

William Shakespeare (1564–1616) was England's greatest poet and playwright. He was born in Stratford-upon-Avon, the son of a well-to-do glove-maker – an important man in the town. At 18, William married a local girl (Anne Hathaway) [or – Anne Hathaway –] but soon left Stratford to seek his fortune in London – England's capital city.

 Step 3 Show who's talking

Pages 10–11: The teacher asked, "Which is the farthest away – China or the sun?"
"China," answered Milly.
"Why do you think that?" asked the teacher in surprise.
"Well, you can see the sun, but you can't see China," Milly replied.

Position and wording of reporting clauses may vary. The following is one example only:
"How's my singing coming on, Miss Jones?" asked Sam.
"I think you should be on TV," replied Miss Jones.
"Really?" said Sam. "You mean I'm good enough for that?"
"No, but if you were on TV I could switch you off," groaned Miss Jones.

 Step 4 Use adjectives and adverbs

Pages 12–13: The little black and white dog was growling playfully.
The enormous guard dog was growling fiercely.

Pages 14–15: Children write their own adjectives and adverbs to complete the sentences.

 Step 5 Improve your vocabulary

Pages 16–17: various means **different**
distort means **twist out of shape**

crisis means **a very difficult time**
an optimist is **someone who expects good things to happen**
chronic means **going on for a long time**
competent means **good at what you are doing**
deceive means **cheat, lie to someone**
pessimist means **someone who expects bad things to happen**

The man suffered for years with a **chronic** illness.
Bad weather can sometimes **distort** the picture on the TV screen.
The wolf tried to **deceive** Little Red Riding Hood, but she saw through his plan.

'Twixt optimist and pessimist,
The difference is droll:
The **optimist** sees the doughnut,
The **pessimist** sees the hole!

 Step 6 Take care with apostrophes

Pages 18–19: The **stall** belonging to the **man** = the man's stall.
The bag belonging to the woman = **the woman's bag.**
The **tail** belonging to the dog = **the dog's tail.**

The pet belonging to Mark = **Mark's pet.**
The wing belonging to the bird = **the bird's wing.**
The idea belonging to Rachel = **Rachel's idea.**

The queen's ✔ cat's ✗ were yowling in the yard.
We had burger's ✗ and chips at Ian's ✔ party.
The farmer's ✔ potatoes were stored in sack's ✗.
Hundred's ✗ of people were at the ship's ✔ launch.

Short form	Long form	Letters missed out
haven't	have not	o
doesn't	does not	o
couldn't	could not	o
would've	would have	ha
didn't	did not	o
might've	might have	ha
I've	I have	ha
we'll	we will	wi
you're	you are	a
it's	it is	i

Step 7 Get your facts in order

Check your child's written instructions to make sure that they are clear and include appropriate linking words.

Step 8 Keep to the standard

Pages 22–23: Jake was **disappointed** when his team lost the game.
I'm **very pleased** about my exam result.
Emma looks **very fashionable** in her new clothes.
There was an **enormous** parcel in the hall.
Will went home because he felt **ill**.

The group played **brilliantly**.
Why do you always shout **really loudly**?
Everyone should sit **quietly** and wait.
Get ready **quickly** or you'll be late.
My dad and I go out every Saturday.
You and I should see the team.

Step 9 Choose the right style

Pages 24–28: formal letter style – full address in top right-hand corner
full date under address
start: Dear Sir/Madam/Mr.../Mrs.../Ms...
sign off: Yours sincerely/Yours faithfully
informal letter style – shortened address
short form of date
start: Dear... and the person's first name
sign off: Best wishes/Love/Cheers – or whatever you like!

formal language – lots of long words
words written out in full
long sentences
sounds less chatty than everyday speech
main punctuation – full stops and commas

informal language – mostly shorter words
shortened forms like **I'm, wasn't** and so on
short, snappy sentences
sounds like everyday speech
more use of dashes and exclamation marks

Step 10 Proofread your work

Pages 28–29: The following is a **sample** of corrected text only. Different children may correct it in different ways (perhaps adding extra words, or choosing different punctuation marks). As long as the text makes sense, and punctuation is used as explained on pages 6–9, work should be marked correct.

> CAKE CRISIS – SHOCK HORROR!
> All readers will know Mr Jones, Newtown's popular baker. Mr Jones has a problem – he hasn't got anyone to mind his shop when he goes on holiday next week. If he doesn't find someone there will be no bread or cakes on sale all week. If you would like to take over Mr Jones's shop please write to him at 11 High Street, Newtown.